THE INTERNET SAFETY HANDBOOK

INVESTIGATE!

I0893696

ONLINE GAMING

BY CHARLEY LIGHT

Enslow PUBLISHING

Please visit our website, www.enslow.com. For a free color catalog of all our high-quality books, call toll free 1-800-398-2504 or fax 1-877-980-4454.

Library of Congress Cataloging-in-Publication Data
Names: Light, Charley, author.
Title: Online gaming / Charley Light.
Description: Buffalo, New York : Enslow Publishing, [2024] | Series: The internet safety handbook | Includes bibliographical references and index.
Identifiers: LCCN 2023009603 | ISBN 9781978535169 (library binding) | ISBN 9781978535152 (paperback) | ISBN 9781978535176 (ebook)
Subjects: LCSH: Video games–Juvenile literature. | Internet–Safety measures–Juvenile literature. | Video games–Social aspects–Juvenile literature. | Video games and children–Juvenile literature.
Classification: LCC GV1469.3 .L545 2024 | DDC 794.8–dc23/eng/20230308
LC record available at https://lccn.loc.gov/2023009603

Published in 2024 by
Enslow Publishing
2544 Clinton Street
Buffalo, NY 14224

Copyright © 2024 Enslow Publishing

Portions of this work were originally authored by Bonnie Spivet and published as *Playing Games Online*. All new material in this edition authored by Charley Light.

Special thanks to Tobi Fowler for their input in this book.

Designer: Jen Schoembs
Editor: Charley Light

Photo credits: Cover (Boy), p. 1 (Boy) WESTOCK PRODUCTIONS/Shutterstock.com; cover (background), p. 1, series art (background) kerly chonglor/Shutterstock.com; p. 5 Roa-Z3/Shutterstock.com; p. 7 Tkgd2007/JohnnyMrNinja/commons.wikimedia.org; p. 9 KeongDaGreat/Shutterstock.com; p. 11 Natsia27/Shutterstock.com; p. 13 Diego Thomazini/Shutterstock.com; p. 15 Prostock-studio/Shutterstock.com; p. 17 Ivanko80/Shutterstock.com; p. 19 Aleksandar Malivuk/Shutterstock.com; p. 23 Monkey Business Images/Shutterstock.com; p. 25 aslysun/Shutterstock.com; p. 27 Gorodenkoff/Shutterstock.com; p. 29 Pixel-Shot/Shutterstock.com.

All rights reserved. No part of this book may be reproduced in any form without permission in writing from the publisher, except by a reviewer.

Some of the images in this book illustrate individuals who are models. The depictions do not imply actual situations or events.

Printed in the United States of America

CPSIA compliance information: Batch #CSENS24: For further information contact Enslow Publishing at 1-800-398-2504.

Find us on

CONTENTS

Words in the glossary appear in **bold** type the first time they are used in the text.

LET'S PLAY!

The following quests have been completed: *Handle the Homework, Conquer the Chores, Devour the Dinner.* New quest unlocked: *Get Ready to Game!*

With permission from your guardians, you and your friends are ready to game together online. Will you work as a team to take down fearsome monsters? Or will you duel to the (virtual) death in a fighting game? Maybe you'll see who can craft the rarest item, catch the shiniest creature, or build the coolest castle. Whatever you play, add this book to your **inventory** to serve as your online gaming guide.

EXPLORE MORE

Games from major companies can cost around $70 when they come out. Buying used devices and games can help save money. You might even be able to play games at your local library or rent them for free!

Lots of gamers customize their gear. What does your dream gaming setup look like?

GRAB YOUR GEAR

To play games online, you need a gaming device. Different games require different devices. Mobile games can be played on smartphones and tablets. You can also play games on personal computers, or PCs. You can even build your own PC especially for gaming!

Consoles are special computers for playing video games that usually connect to a TV. The Sony PlayStation 5, XBox Series X and Series S, and the Nintendo Switch are the most current gaming consoles. The Switch can also be played in handheld mode.

EXPLORE MORE

Cross-platform games let you and your friends play online together even if you're using different devices. Games such as *Among Us* can be played from a smartphone, tablet, PC, or console.

The Entertainment Software Rating Board (ESRB) gives games ratings based on their content.

ESRB GAME RATINGS

RATING:	Who Can Play
EVERYONE	all ages
EVERYONE 10+	ages 10 and up
TEEN	teens 13 and up
MATURE 17+	ages 17 and up
ADULTS ONLY 18+	ages 18 and up

GAMING ON THE GO

Mobile games can be played on mobile devices such as smartphones and tablets. They can be downloaded from Apple's App Store or Android's Google Play store. **Browser** games are played on websites.

Many mobile and browser games have a free version and a paid version. The free version will have limited features. The game creator hopes players will get hooked and then spend money to play more. Never spend money online without asking a guardian first. If you aren't careful, free-to-play games can turn into pay-to-play games. They can really cost you!

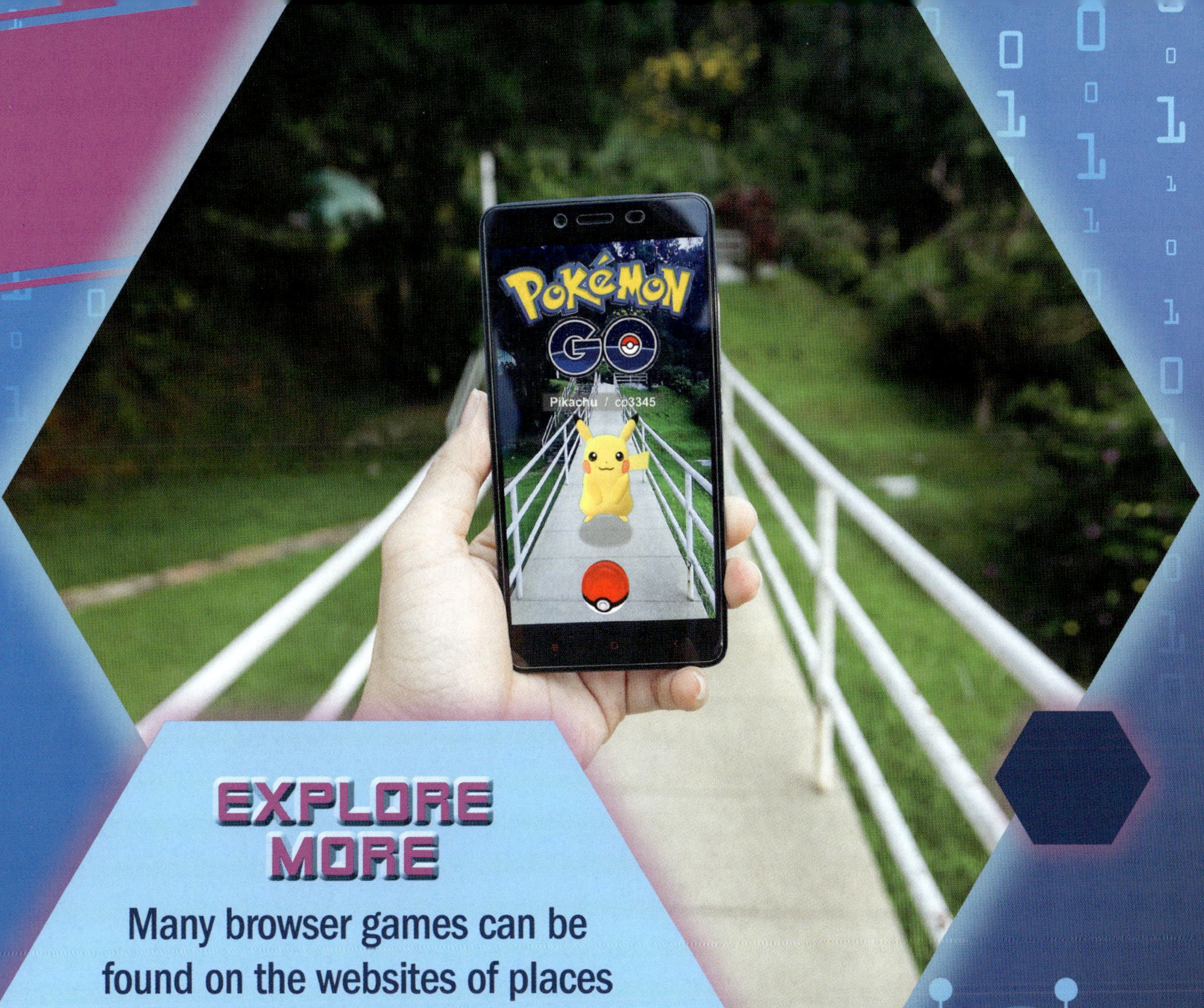

Mobile games such as Pokémon GO *blend online gaming with the real world!*

EXPLORE MORE

Many browser games can be found on the websites of places such as zoos and museums. Others are on sites just for games, such as Knowledge Adventure and Funbrain. Both are full of fun, casual games that teach reading and math skills.

MULTIPLAYER MADNESS

Multiplayer games are played by two or more people. Players might work together as a team, or they might be **opponents** competing against one another. Some games have multiple modes you can play in.

Offline multiplayer games are often called "couch co-op" because you have to be together in person—maybe on the same couch—to play! Other multiplayer games can be played online with gamers around the globe. Sometimes you can choose friends to play with. Other times the game pairs you up with players you don't know.

EXPLORE MORE

Some multiplayer games online have a voice chat feature that lets players talk to each other. Other games have only text chat. Some have only kid-friendly pre-written texts you can choose from. Those are the safest for kids to use.

Super Smash Bros. *on Nintendo Switch can be played as couch co-op or online with friends or random opponents.*

M-M-WHOA!

Massive multiplayer online games (MMOs) have thousands to millions of players. In MMOs, players make characters called avatars. They use their avatars to chat and play with other gamers.

Some MMOs are about crafting and building. Others are shooting and fighting games. In role-playing (RPG) MMOs, you also use your avatar to play an adventure game. You can often buy things for your avatars, such as clothing, gear, or even homes, using in-game money. You can spend real money to get in-game money. Some MMOs also require paid **subscriptions** to play.

EXPLORE MORE

In 2022, 67 percent of all *Roblox* players were under 16. As of 2023, *Roblox* has over 43 million players every day! Most people play *Roblox* on a phone. This game is available to play in over 22 countries.

Roblox *(above),* Minecraft, School of Dragons, Pirate101, Wizard101, *and* Star Stable *are MMOs with many younger players.*

MAKING ACCOUNTS

You usually need an account to play games online. You'll need a guardian's permission and help for this part.

Making an account includes creating a username. It's like your nametag online. You'll also need a password, which is the key to open your account. Usually, you also need a guardian's email. Never put private personal information in a username, password, or profile online. Don't use your real name or nickname where other players will see it. Don't use personal numbers like your age or birthday, either.

Playing games together is a great way for you and your guardian to talk about online gaming safety.

EXPLORE MORE

PlayStation Plus, XBox Game Pass, and Nintendo Switch Online are all subscription services that cost money. They allow gamers to play a **rotating** selection of games for a monthly or yearly price. It's like Netflix for games.

PLAY IT SAFE

The rules for playing are the same as making your account: Never share private information about yourself online. Some games online include ways to communicate with other players, such as text or voice chat. Never answer personal questions from strangers, even if they seem like fun gaming buddies. Real friends will respect your privacy.

No game is worth risking your safety or privacy for. If you're ever unsure if a game is safe, don't play it. If you ever feel unsafe while playing games online, talk to a trusted adult for help.

Video games can be fun for the whole family.

EXPLORE MORE

Guardians can use parental controls on some gaming devices and accounts. Parental controls can include choosing which games kids can play, how long they can play, controlling internet access, and blocking communication.

WHAT'S YOUR GAMING STYLE?

As long as you're having fun and being kind, there's no wrong way to play. If you're looking for a good story, you might like role-playing games (RPGs). "Sandbox" games are good for exploring and crafting. Fighting games are great for competition.

Competitive gaming is trying to be the best at a game. This can include playing in **tournaments** online or in person and sharing scores online to see who is at the top. Social gaming is a way to have fun with friends! You can play anything just for fun.

EXPLORE MORE

Completionist gamers like to finish every single part of a game, not just the main story. Speedrunners try to beat a game as quickly as possible, sometimes while following rules set by the game's community—not the game itself!

You can have a combination of different gaming styles!

GOOD GAMING MANNERS

Having a sporting attitude is key in and out of the game. Sporting means being fair, respectful, and kind no matter how the game goes. Gamers often say "GG" (which stands for "good game") to their team and opponents after playing, whether they have won or lost! This keeps things positive for everyone.

Some people cyberbully players who are new to online games. Cyberbullying is using digital technology to hurt someone on purpose. You can choose to be kind and offer to teach new players the ropes.

GAMER SPEAK

AFK: away from keyboard
BRB: be right back
GG: good game
GL: good luck
GLHF: good luck have fun
NT: nice try
TY: thank you
YW: you're welcome
WB: welcome back
WP: well played

These are some common abbreviations used in the online gaming community!

EXPLORE MORE

Feeling upset after a loss is often called being "tilted" in the online gaming community. Playing while tilted can make things worse. It's always okay to take a break from the game if you feel upset in any way.

NOT-SO-GOOD GRIEF

Griefing is a form of cyberbullying that happens in online gaming. People who are griefing are playing online games to purposefully bother other players. They mess up a game, break rules, bully others, and make trouble for other gamers. Griefing ruins the game for everybody.

If someone griefs you, you may feel angry or hurt. However, don't strike back. Tell a trusted adult what has happened. **Report** the problem and **block** the player. Never blame yourself for someone griefing you. Don't feel bad for reporting cyberbullying. You're helping keep the game fun and safe.

EXPLORE MORE

Griefing includes playing the game in a way it wasn't intended to be played. Hurting your own teammates on purpose, giving your own team false information, and working with the opposing team to bring down your own team are all forms of griefing.

People who are griefing may try to get you to "rage quit," or stop playing the game because you're upset.

PROFESSIONAL GAMING

Professional gamers are esports athletes who make money from playing games. They play in tournaments online or in person. Kids and teens can compete in some competitive gaming tournaments too. The Digital Schoolhouse Junior Tournament is for gamers ages 8 to 11 in the United Kingdom. This tournament lets kids try out real jobs in the gaming industry.

There are also coaches and team managers who help esports athletes play their best. Journalists cover esports news. Commentators narrate competitive games as they are played. Analysts talk about professional games afterward to explain what happened.

EXPLORE MORE

Professional esports athletes take care of all parts of their health to play their very best. This includes taking breaks from the game! It also means getting enough sleep, eating well, drinking water, and moving their bodies.

Some esports teams represent, or stand for, a whole country.

GAMING CONTENT CREATORS

Gaming content creators make content, such as YouTube videos, about video games. Streamers are content creators who perform in real time for their audience online. Gaming streamers play video games and usually talk to their audience while they play. The audience can talk back through text chat. Many gamers stream on Twitch.

"Let's Play!" videos, walk-throughs, and reviews are other popular kinds of gaming content. Let's Play! videos show the content creator playing a game while narrating. Walkthroughs teach others how to play a game. Reviews share a content creator's thoughts on a game.

Many professionals in the gaming community have many jobs, like competing and streaming.

EXPLORE MORE

Streamers and gaming content creators need special gear. Both usually start with a computer, an internet connection, a camera, a microphone, and, of course—games to play! Streamers also need **software** to stream their games. A video capture device records gameplay.

GG!

Quest *Get Ready to Game* is complete! But that's just the beginning of your journey. The world of online gaming is an ever-changing, constantly growing place. There's always more to explore. Maybe you'll even build a career here someday!

In the meantime, GLHF! Whether you're goofing around in a sandbox or competing at the highest level in front of an audience, the goal is to have a good time with friends. Gaming online is a chance to connect with others, so keep it kind and sign off with a GG!

EXPLORE MORE

Gaming safely can help you grow important skills for life. You're learning how to work with others, handle stress, solve problems creatively, multitask, and so much more. In many games, you'll even learn how to manage money!

Friendships you make through gaming can last a lifetime.

GLOSSARY

block: To turn on a setting that stops another user from being able to see your profile or talk to you.

browser: A program for finding and reading websites on the internet.

inventory: A place to store things you can carry with you in a game.

opponent: A person or team you must beat to win a game.

report: Telling a website that another user is behaving harmfully.

rotating: Coming in and out on a schedule.

software: A computer code, or program, that instructs a computer what to do.

subscription: A service where you make payments at set times in order to receive or access products.

tournament: A series of contests testing the skill of many athletes in the same sport.

FOR MORE INFORMATION

BOOKS

Beam, Bjorn. *Security Squad: Your Kid's Playbook to Cybersecurity, Cyberbullying, and Coding!* Madrid, ES: Beam Reach Ventures, 2019.

Garland, Ian. *Coding for Minecrafters: Unofficial Adventures for Kids Learning Computer Code.* New York, NY: Sky Pony Press, 2019.

Scholastic. *Level Up 2023: An AFK Book.* New York, NY: Scholastic Inc., 2023.

WEBSITES

Funbrain
www.funbrain.com
Learn while you play these fun browser games!

Knowledge Adventure
www.knowledgeadventure.com
You can play even more educational games here!

PBS Kids
pbskids.org/games
Play learning games with characters from PBS!

Publisher's note to educators and parents: Our editors have carefully reviewed these websites to ensure that they are suitable for students. Many websites change frequently, however, and we cannot guarantee that a site's future contents will continue to meet our high standards of quality and educational value. Be advised that students should be closely supervised whenever they access the internet.

INDEX